GPJC
6/19

CINCINNATI
REDS

STARS, STATS, HISTORY, AND MORE!

BY K. C. KELLEY

Published by The Child's World®
1980 Lookout Drive • Mankato, MN 56003-1705
800-599-READ • www.childsworld.com

ISBN 9781503828209
LCCN 2018944833

Printed in the United States of America
PAO2392

About the Author

K.C. Kelley is a huge sports
fan who has written more
than 100 books for kids. His
favorite sport is baseball.
He has also written about
football, basketball, soccer,
and even auto racing! He lives
in Santa Barbara, California.

On the Cover

Main photo: First baseman
Joey Votto
Inset: Hall of Fame catcher
Johnny Bench

CONTENTS

GO, REDS!

Baseball has a long history. People have been playing the game since the early part of the 1800s. Only a few teams from those days are still around. The Cincinnati Reds are one of them. This famous team has been a part of baseball for more than 150 years! Today's Reds carry on the **tradition**. The team's fans hope they see another trophy in the team's case. Let's meet the Reds!

Speedy Reds outfielder Billy Hamilton is one ➤
of the fastest players in baseball.

WHO ARE THE REDS?

The Reds play in the National League (NL). That group is part of Major League Baseball (MLB). MLB also includes the American League (AL). There are 30 teams in MLB. The winner of the NL plays the winner of the AL in the **World Series**. The Reds of the 1970s were awesome. Cincinnati has had some good teams since then, too. Will another World Series come soon?

◄ *Second baseman Scooter Gennett has become a surprise home run hero!*

WHERE THEY CAME FROM

I n 1869, the first pro baseball team was called the Cincinnati Red Stockings. Later, that Red Stockings team played in the American Association from 1882 to 1889. Then, in 1890, that team dropped "Stockings" and joined the National League. The Reds have been a part of the NL ever since.

John "Bid" McPhee starred for the Reds from 1882 to 1899. ➤

JOHN McPHEE, 2d B. Cincinnati

COPYRIGHTED BY GOODWIN & CO. 1888.

OLD JUDGE
CIGARETTES.
GOODWIN & CO., New York.

WHO THEY PLAY

The Reds play in the NL Central Division. The other teams in the NL Central are the Chicago Cubs, the Milwaukee Brewers, the Pittsburgh Pirates, and the St. Louis Cardinals. The Reds play more games against their division **rivals** than against other teams. In all, the Reds play 162 games each season. They play 81 games at home and 81 on the road.

◄ *Cincinnati's Rafael Iglesias is one of the top relief pitchers in the NL.*

WHERE THEY PLAY

Cincinnati's Great American Ballpark opened in 2003. It was built on the banks of the Ohio River. Behind the centerfield wall, a huge scoreboard is topped with smokestacks. Old-time riverboats had smokestacks like these. The tall towers light up and send out smoke and fireworks when the Reds hit a home run.

The smokestacks at the Great American Ballpark ➤ tower over fans in the outfield seats.

CINCINNATI

PNC
POWER STACKS

RED HITS SIGN, FAN WINS
TOYOTA

TOYOTA · TOYOTA · TOYOTA · TOYOTA

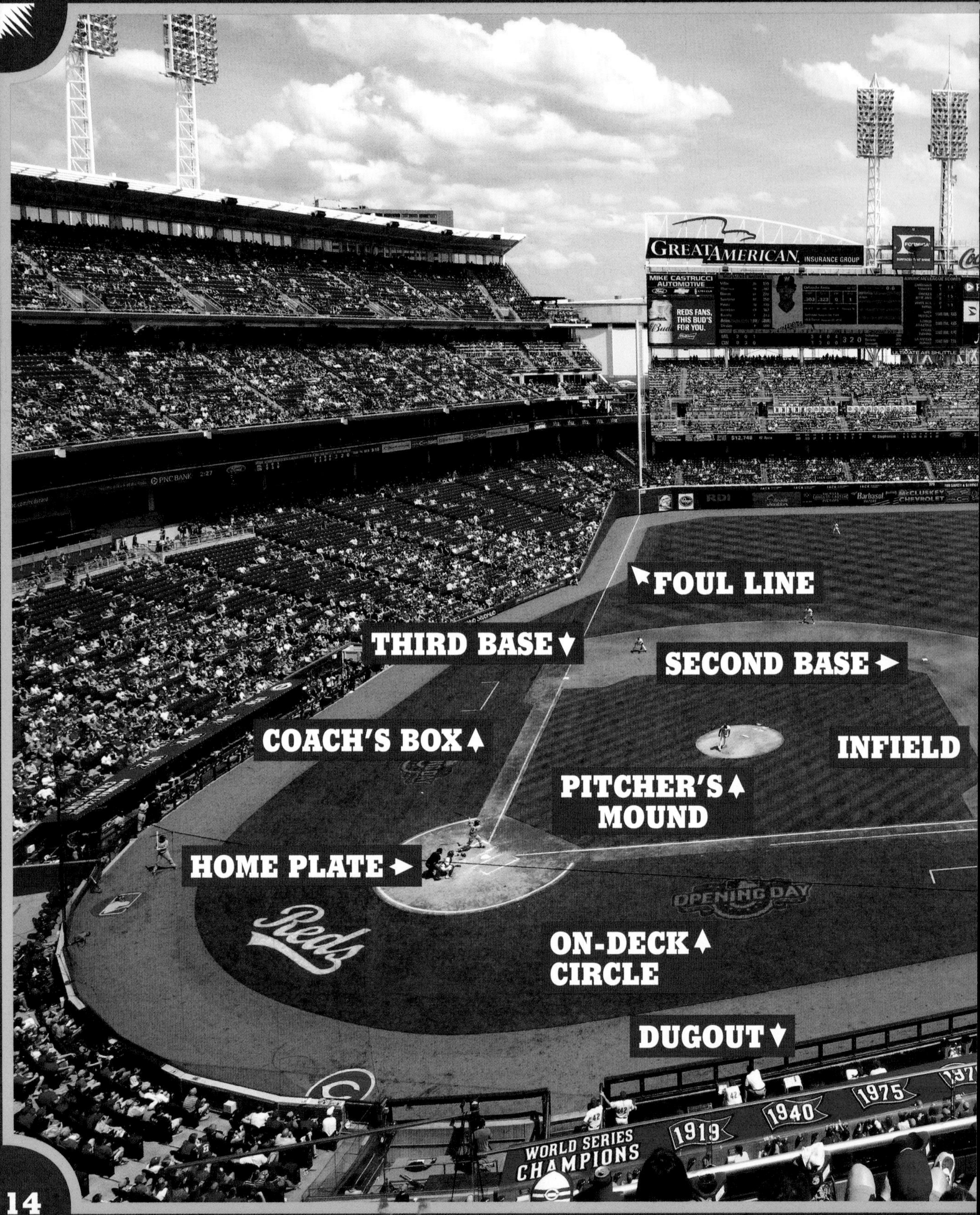

FOUL LINE

THIRD BASE ▾

SECOND BASE ▸

COACH'S BOX ▴

INFIELD

PITCHER'S ▴ MOUND

HOME PLATE ▸

ON-DECK ▴ CIRCLE

DUGOUT ▾

THE BASEBALL FIELD

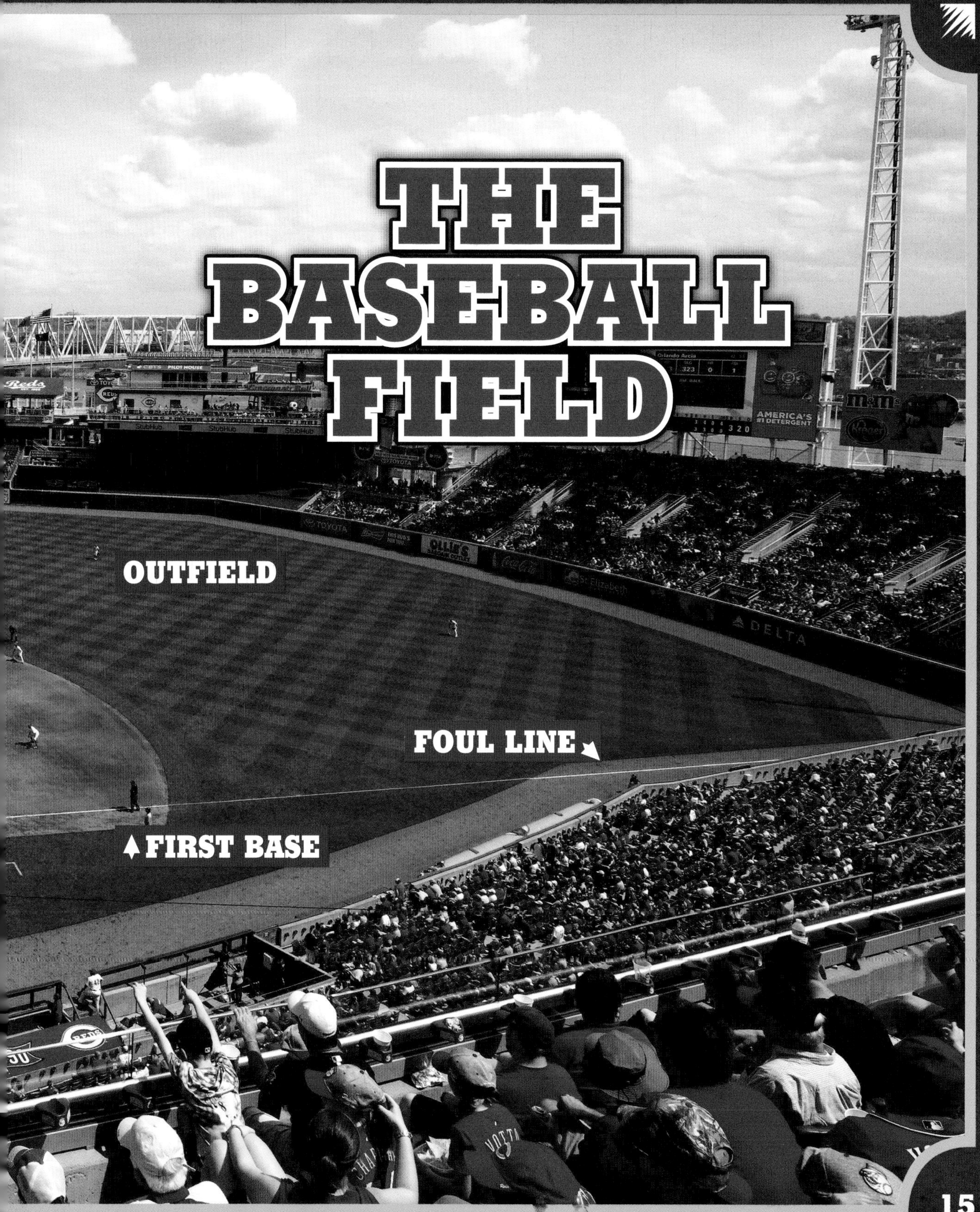

OUTFIELD

FOUL LINE ◤

▲ FIRST BASE

BIG DAYS

The Reds have had a lot of great days in their long history. Here are a few of them.

1975—The Reds of the 1970s were among baseball's best teams ever. "The Big Red Machine" won the World Series this year and in 1976.

1988—Tom Browning did not allow a baserunner to the Los Angeles Dodgers. That was a **perfect game**! It was only the twelfth "perfecto" pitched in MLB history.

The 1975 Reds danced on the field after they won the World Series. ➤

1990—The Reds returned to the top of the baseball world. They won four straight games over the Oakland A's. It was Cincinnati's fifth World Series title.

TOUGH DAYS

Like every team, the Reds have had some not-so-great days, too. Here are a few their fans might not want to recall.

1964—The Reds traded star outfielder Frank Robinson to the Baltimore Orioles. He won the **MVP** for his new team and made six All-Star teams!

1982—The Reds reached a new low this season. The team lost 101 games. That was the most in Cincinnati's long history.

2018—This Reds team had the worst start in team history. They won only three of their first 21 games!

Scooter Gennett heads to the bench after striking out in 2018. ➤

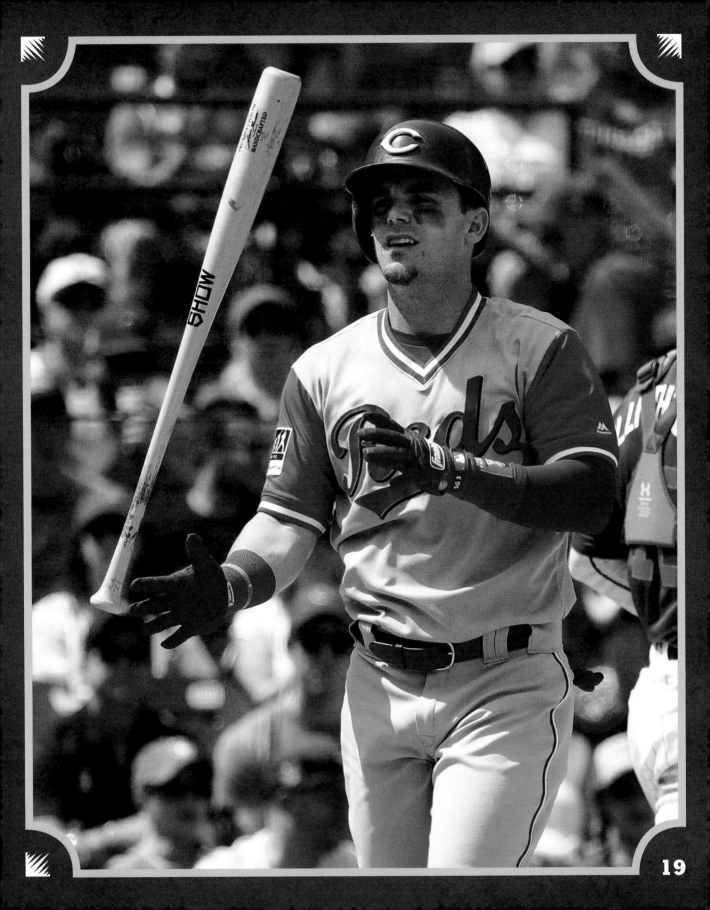

MEET THE FANS!

Reds fans are very loyal. They keep cheering even when their team is struggling. They have fun at the ballpark, too. Four **mascots** help the fans cheer. Mr. Redlegs has a big mustache and a hat from the 1890s. Mr. Red has a modern baseball head. Rosie Red joins the others in a Mascot Race each game. The goofy orange Gapper makes kids laugh!

◀ *Mr. Redlegs and Rosie Red met with Gapper before a Reds game.*

HEROES THEN

Some of baseball's greatest players have been Reds. Johnny Bench is probably the best catcher in history. Second baseman Joe Morgan knocked homers and stole lots of bases. Pete Rose had more hits than any player in MLB history. Tony Perez was a hard-hitting first baseman. These four players were part of the great Reds teams of the 1970s.

Johnny Bench won two Most Valuable Player awards. ➤
He also earned 10 Gold Gloves for great defense.

HEROES NOW

First baseman Joey Votto has been a star for the Reds since he joined the team in 2007. His hitting and leadership help the team win. Second baseman Scooter Gennett has become one of the top hitters in the NL. Speedy Billy Hamilton might be the fastest player in the league. Third baseman Eugenio Suárez is a solid young player.

◆ *Joey Votto has been named to six All-Star teams in his years with the Reds.*

GEARING UP

Baseball players wear team uniforms. On defense, they wear leather gloves to catch the ball. As batters, they wear hard helmets. This protects them from pitches. Batters hit the ball with long wood bats. Each player chooses his own size of bat. Catchers have the toughest job. They wear a lot of protection.

THE BASEBALL

The outside of the Major League baseball is made from cow leather. Two leather pieces shaped like 8's are stitched together. There are 108 stitches of red thread. These stitches help players grip the ball. Inside, the ball has a small center of cork and rubber. Hundreds of feet of yarn are tightly wound around this center.

CATCHER'S HELMET

CHEST PROTECTOR

WRIST BANDS

CATCHER'S MITT

CATCHER'S MASK

SHIN GUARDS

CATCHER'S GEAR

TEAM STATS

H ere are some of the all-time career records for the Cincinnati Reds. All these stats are through the 2018 regular season.

HOME RUNS	
Johnny Bench	389
Frank Robinson	324

RBI	
Johnny Bench	1,376
Tony Perez	1,192

BATTING AVERAGE	
Cy Seymour	.332
Edd Roush	.331

HITS	
Pete Rose	3,358
Barry Larkin	2,340

WINS	
Eppa Rixey	179
Tony Mullane	163

STRIKEOUTS	
Jim Maloney	1,592
Mario Soto	1,449

Hall of Fame second baseman Joe Morgan ➤
was a great hitter and base-stealer.

STOLEN BASES

Bid McPhee	568
Joe Morgan	406

GLOSSARY

mascot (MASS-cot) a costumed character who helps fans cheer

MVP Most Valuable Player, an award given to the top player in each league

perfect game (PUR-fekt GAYM) a game in which the pitcher does not allow a single opponent to reach base

rival (RYE-vuhl) two people or groups competing for the same thing

tradition (trah-DISH-un) anything that people have done or believed for a long time

World Series (WURLD SEE-reez) the annual championship of Major League Baseball

FIND OUT MORE

IN THE LIBRARY

Connery-Boyd, Peg. *Cincinnati Reds: The Big Book of Activities*. Chicago, IL: Sourcebooks/Jabberwocky, 2016.

Gilbert, Sara. *World Series Champions: Cincinnati Reds*. Mankato, MN: Creative Paperbacks, 2013.

Sports Illustrated for Kids (Editors). *Big Book of Who: Baseball*. New York, NY: Sports Illustrated Kids, 2017.

ON THE WEB

Visit our website for links about the Cincinnati Reds:
childsworld.com/links

Note to Parents, Teachers, and Librarians: We routinely verify our Web links to make sure they are safe and active sites. So encourage your readers to check them out!

INDEX